Startup Capital

B. Vincent

Published by RWG Publishing, 2021.

STARTUP CAPITAL

First edition. June 23, 2021.

Written by B. Vincent.

Also by B. Vincent

Affiliate Marketing
Affiliate Marketing
Affiliate Marketing

Standalone
Affiliate Recruiting
Business Layoffs & Firings
Business and Entrepreneur Guide
Business Remote Workforce
Career Transition
Project Management
Precision Targeting
Professional Development
Strategic Planning
Content Marketing
Imminent List Building
Getting Past GateKeepers
Banner Ads
Bookkeeping

Bridge Pages
Business Acquisition
Business Bogging
Marketing Automation
Better Meetings
Conversion Optimization
Creative Solutions
Employee Recruitment
Startup Capital

Table of Contents

Startup Capital.. 1
Module 1: Introduction to Startup capital............................ 3
Module 2: Investors.. 11
Module 3: Alternatives 15
Conclusion.. 19

Startup Capital

Hello, and welcome to this course on Startup Capital. In this course, we're going to cover how to raise capital for your business. This course is divided into 3 modules.

1. Module 1 covers various types of loan options.

1. Module 2 goes over investor capital.

1. Module 3 covers a variety of alternatives.

By the time this course is over, you'll know how to effectively find and raise funds for your startup. So, without further ado, let's dive into the first module.

OK, guys, welcome to Module 1. In this module, our expert will give us an overview of bank loans. So get ready to take some notes. And let's jump right in.

Module 1: Introduction to Startup capital

Bringing your business idea into life is easier said than done. At the end of the day, you have to understand that experience plays a major role in making that great idea work. If you're unfamiliar with the ins and outs of starting a small business, turning your dream into reality can be challenging.

Simply put, starting a business involves several factors including staff, location, inventories, suppliers, startup costs, and more.

However, these factors can only be put into consideration once you've secured startup capital.

In this training, you'll learn about the different options for small business to raise capital. In Module 1, we'll look at the different types of loans.

Module 2, we'll focus on investors and how to choose the right one for you.

Finally, module 3 will provide you practical alternatives to raise capital from within your community.

To start things off, let's take a look at the types of loans that a small business can apply for

Bank Loans:

If you're just starting out, then this may seem to be the best option for you in securing capital. It's a logical and practical steps to take given that bank loans often have the lowest interest rates.

There are two main types of bank loans: fixed and flexible.

Fixed Bank Loans refer to loans that have an agreed payment schedule and a defined interest rate.

On the other hand, **Flexible Bank Loans** are loans that have adaptable rates. The rates are determined depending on your business and financial needs.

With either type of loan, the repayment term can be between 1 and 15 years, depending on the loan amount. Interest rates range from 7% to 12%, but can be subject to change depending on a variety of factors, such as the loan amount and current market conditions.

However, securing a bank loan can be very daunting for small businesses. This is because banks have drastically reduced their loan approval rate. Citing failure is the main reason.

For a bank loan to be approved, you need to comply with a number of requirements.

These include: credit history, financial statements, collateral, cash flow, and of course, business experience.

These requirements are vital when it comes to securing your loan. secured loan, as the name implies, requires that you offer an asset or security that the bank can seize if your company fails to repay in an agreed timeframe.

Although secured loans offer higher amounts and lower interest rates, they can only be secured by companies with significant assets.

In short, applying for bank loans is a tough choice for small businesses.

SBA Loans:

The Small Business Administration, or SBA, is a cabinet level federal agency in the US that offers extensive assistance to small businesses describing their purpose. This is what their website has to say.

The SBA is the only cabinet level federal agency "**fully dedicated to small business and provides counseling, capital and contracting expertise as the nation's only go to resource and voice for small businesses**".

SBA does not offer loans, but instead it works with its partnering lenders, community development organizations, and micro lending institutions.

To ensure protection for both borrowers and lenders. All lenders are subject to verification, and all loans should meet certain conditions to be approved.

SBA loans are only available to businesses around the US or its territories that do not have any other means of securing startup capital.

The SBA offers 4 kinds of loans:

1. 7(a) loans.

1. Micro loans.

1. 504 loans.

1. Disaster loans.

Each of these loans has specific uses. When applying for one of them, you must state what you plan to do with the money.

7 (a) Loan:

A general small business loan, commonly known as a 7(a) loan is the most common type of SBA loan and has the widest range of uses.

It includes financial help for businesses with special requirements.

7(a) loans can be used for startup costs, purchasing land and real estate equipment, refinancing debt and more.

To become eligible, businesses must:

- operate for profit.

- engaged in the US.

- Have reasonable owner equity to invest

- and use alternative financial resources such as personal assets.

$5 million is the maximum loan amount with no minimum amount.

Interest rates are negotiated between the borrowers and the lender, but should meet the SBA maximums or conditions.

Micro Loan:

The Micro Loan Program is a type of SBA loan that is typically used to start or expand a new business, including nonprofit community based organizations such as childcare centers.

Micro loans cannot be used to pay existing debts or purchase real estate.

Eligibility depends on the intermediary lenders own lending and credit requirements. However, most intermediaries will require some type of collateral and personal guarantee of the business owner.

Interest rates for micro loans are between 8% and 13%, having six years as the maximum repayment term

504 Loan:

A real estate and equipment loan more commonly known as a 504 loan program is a type of SBA loan that is used to finance a startup business while promoting business growth and job creation.

504 loan funds can be used for different purchases such as existing buildings or land and land improvements.

It's also used to fund the construction or renovation of facilities.

504 loan funds are also used for refinancing debt for business expansions.

The 504 loan program offers both immediate and long term benefits that business owners can surely take advantage of.

Top Level benefits include:

- 90% financing

- fixed rate interest rates

- longer loan amortization

- no balloon payments

- and improved cash flow resulting in more savings.

In order to qualify for this loan your business must be operated for profit and should comply with the size standards set by the SBA.

You should have tangible net worth of more than $15 million and an average net income of $5 million or less for the preceding two years prior to application.

The maximum loan amount is $5 million but small manufacturers or energy projects may qualify for $5.5 million debenture.

Small businesses and lenders can contact a Certified Development Company or CDC in their area for more additional application requirements.

Disaster Loan:

A Disaster Loan is a low interest loan provided by the SBA designed to help businesses and homeowners recover from declared disasters.

There are four types of disaster loans:

- Physical damage loans.

- Mitigation assistance.

- Economic injury disaster loans

- and military reservists' loans.

To be eligible for a disaster loan business of all sizes must be located in declared disaster areas and have been affected by declared disasters including civil unrest and natural disasters, such as: hurricanes, flooding, earthquakes, wildfires and even pandemics.

Disaster loans can be used for: working capital or financing normal operating expenses, paying losses not covered by insurance, or funding from the Federal Emergency Management Agency, FEMA, as well as paying business operating expenses that could have been met had the disaster not occurred.

Module 2: Investors

Securing investment as a small business has a fine line between extremely easy and incredibly difficult.

Investors-individuals or firms that you can reach out to and impress with your promising mission, they can provide you the assistance you need to raise capital.

However, it's important to note that most investors often have less money to spare than larger institutions.

To secure an investor, you need to know how and why they work.

This module will clearly explain that.

Venture Capitalists:

Venture Capitalists are investors, usually a professionally managed firm that invests other people's money on their behalf.

They obtained capital from a range of sources including pension funds, insurance companies and other investors.

Venture Capitalists invest in small companies that they know will provide higher returns.

Venture Capitalists are not interested in companies that want to work on a small scale. Rather, they're willing to fund a business that has a bright future of becoming the next industry Titan.

Investing in a small business is risky, so venture capitalists expect a high return, equity in the company, access to financial records, and to say in large decisions.

From their standpoint, being involved in these things make their investment worthwhile. Due to their extensive professional experience some small businesses bring venture capitalists on board not only for investment, but also for their financial advice.

However, this can be a tough decision for those who want to keep in charge of their business.

The best way to grab the attention of a venture capitalist is to be referred to them by a financial professional, such as a banker or accountant.

Angel Investors:

An Angel Investor, also known as a private investor, is a wealthy individual who can provide financial assistance to startups by investing their money in exchange for a share in the company.

They usually provide a one-time investment to help the business get started.

In some cases, one angel investor can single handedly provide capital that no other investors are needed.

However, most of the time, they are composed of a group of people that collectively support a startup.

The biggest difference between venture capitalists and angel investors is that:

Angel investors invest their own capital. This means that they are willing to put their money at risk.

Another significant difference between the two, the angels aren't entirely motivated by profit.

They are more likely to be inspired by a great pitch and back a company because they want to see it succeed rather than simply because they think they'll get a higher return.

Compared to other lenders, angel investors are more laid back when it comes to making terms.

They typically expect less control in the company than Venture Capitalists.

Instead, they are looking for a share in the company that they believe will thrive in the future.

Angel investors can be divided into 2 categories:

Affiliated and non-affiliated.

Affiliated angels are people that you're already engaged with, that you can reach out to through an appointment or personal meeting. They might be current or former colleagues, entrepreneurs or people in your social circle who invest in their spare time.

On the other hand, **non-affiliated angels** are people that are not part of your network nor are connected with your business. The best ways to find non-affiliated angels include looking through local advertisements, network referrals, and angel investing websites.

If you already know some angels, they will probably be able to introduce you to even more potential investors.

Speaker 1

Alright, welcome to Module 3. In this module, our expert will cover a range of alternative sources of capital. So get ready to take some notes. And let's jump right in

Module 3: Alternatives

Having a business idea means that your friends and family are going to be the first ones to know about it. After all, they might have spent months or maybe even years listening to you talk about your plans, and seeing how you're slowly turning your idea into a reality.

Those close to you may want to support your dreams, but it's important to find the balance between professional and personal matters.

In this module, you will find a few tips for encouraging capital in a healthy and safe way, as well as finding other alternatives.

Gifts:

On the onset, generous friends or relatives may offer you a small cash gift to support you from the first few expenses.

This can be great and be well appreciated. If the intentions are right.

Why is that so?

Well, once the company becomes successful people who you thought were giving you wholehearted gifts are now expecting their money to be repaid.

To avoid such discussions, it's best to clearly communicate to the other person that whatever amount they give is considered as a gift. Not Alone. You can also communicate through writing.

When you clear out these issues, you keep things professional.

Loans:

Friends and family members are less likely to charge you interest than any other source. So this can be a great way to raise money without added expenses.

However, it's important to keep in mind that these loans will probably be way smaller than those from banks or investors.

Another thing to point out once you've borrowed money, your personal spending may be under scrutiny while you're in debt.

It's best to work with a business attorney or a peer to peer lending company, so everything is above board and professional.

Equity:

If you have friends or relatives who believe in your company's potential, they may want to have a share of it.

Like selling equity to an investor, this will not work for people who want to retain full control of their company.

Before choosing a person it's best to consider first, how working with this person as a business partner might affect your personal relationship.

If you decide to sell equity to an individual, make sure to involve a business attorney so everything is official.

Crowdfunding:

Crowdfunding from the word itself is a funding project where you raise money for your business by asking for support from a large number of people or crowd.

Crowdfunding has gained popularity in recent years, with lending platforms like Kickstarter and Indiegogo that have raised a total of more than $34 billion.

When you crowdfund you publicly raise money. This means that you have to clearly explain the reason why you're raising money.

There are 4 types of crowdfunding:

1.   Donation based.

1.   Rewards based.

1.   Debt based.

1.   Equity based.

For example:

You can use rewards based crowdfunding and give your backers unique rewards in exchange for their donations, or use equity based crowdfunding and sell small parts of the company.

However, you do it, the process is formalized through the crowdfunding platform, and will clearly mentioned that the money donated will not be repaid.

So if you're unsure about involving friends and family through other methods, Crowdfunding might be the best option for you.

Credit Card:

Credit cards can provide easy money for small business owners.

There are 2 types of credit cards:

- personal

- and business.

Personal Credit Cards provide better government protection while **Business Cards** provide higher limits, and better rewards such as a discount on office supplies.

This can be really beneficial for business owners.

Funds through credit cards are easily accessible, which can be very helpful for certain transactions. Regardless of what credit card you choose, paying your bills on time is paramount. paying your bills on time means improving your credit score and is beneficial both for the owners and businesses. This also means you can enjoy special rewards and perks such as airline miles, gift cards and cash back.

However, despite the number of benefits that credit cards provide, they also have serious risks involved.

Being unable to pay your bills on time can seriously wreck your personal finances.

Another disadvantage is that credit card interest rates are way higher than traditional loans, which can ultimately lead to bigger debt.

These pricey arrears can drag your business down during tough times.

Conclusion

In reality, turning your business idea into reality isn't easy. Serious funding is involved. You can't think ahead of how prosperous the business can be. If you don't have the means to get things started.

You need to get that first boost to kick things off.

The three main ways you can raise capital are through: loans, investors, and friends and family.

Small businesses may find it difficult to secure a bank loan, but there are groups like the SBA specifically designed to help companies find capital to make their dreams come true.

When it comes to finding investors, each has its own pros and cons, you should first determine what your business needs are, then choose the right one for you, if it's a venture capitalist, or an angel investor. You if you decide to seek help from your friends and family and your company's finances, make it clear that their support is solely for business, and that there are no blurred lines between your personal and professional life. Lastly, if you want to apply for a credit card, remember that you need to accept serious consequences if you're not able to pay your bills on time. These modules provide a list of practical choices to choose from. Choose the ones that best suit your situation. After all, at the end of the day, it's your business and only you know what works best for you.

If you decide to seek help from your friends and family and your company's finances, make it clear that their support is solely for business, and that there are no blurred lines between your personal and professional life.

Lastly, if you want to apply for a credit card, remember that you need to accept serious consequences if you're not able to pay your bills on time.

These modules provide a list of practical choices to choose from.

Choose the ones that best suit your situation.

After all, at the end of the day, it's your business and only you know what works best for you.

Don't miss out!

Visit the website below and you can sign up to receive emails whenever B. Vincent publishes a new book. There's no charge and no obligation.

https://books2read.com/r/B-A-QWUO-LAUPB

BOOKS 2 READ

Connecting independent readers to independent writers.

Also by B. Vincent

Affiliate Marketing
Affiliate Marketing
Affiliate Marketing

Standalone
Affiliate Recruiting
Business Layoffs & Firings
Business and Entrepreneur Guide
Business Remote Workforce
Career Transition
Project Management
Precision Targeting
Professional Development
Strategic Planning
Content Marketing
Imminent List Building
Getting Past GateKeepers
Banner Ads
Bookkeeping

Bridge Pages
Business Acquisition
Business Bogging
Marketing Automation
Better Meetings
Conversion Optimization
Creative Solutions
Employee Recruitment
Startup Capital

About the Publisher

Accepting manuscripts in the most categories. We love to help people get their words available to the world.

Revival Waves of Glory focus is to provide more options to be published. We do traditional paperbacks, hardcovers, audio books and ebooks all over the world. A traditional royalty-based publisher that offers self-publishing options, Revival Waves provides a very author friendly and transparent publishing process, with President Bill Vincent involved in the full process of your book. Send us your manuscript and we will contact you as soon as possible.

Contact: Bill Vincent at rwgpublishing@yahoo.com www.rwgpublishing.com

www.ingramcontent.com/pod-product-compliance
Lightning Source LLC
Chambersburg PA
CBHW030536210326
41597CB00014B/1175